I0800841

IMAGES
of America

CROMWELL

Local historian Charles Collard Adams lived with his wife, Elizabeth Ranney Adams, in this house at the corner of South and Pleasant Streets until his death in 1925. John Sage, husband of Anne Ranney, built the home in 1761; both were descendants of original settlers. The house was passed down in the Ranney family through the female line until the 20th century. This historic home, known as the Ranney-Adams house, was torn down before 1950. (Courtesy of the Cromwell Historical Society.)

On the Cover: Taken about 1890 by Orrin Sage Wightman, this photograph shows the exterior of the 1750 Capt. Daniel Ranney home on Main Street. Ranney was a sea captain who became wealthy in the West Indies trade. The Wightman family owned the home for most of the 19th century. Frederick Butler Wightman, seen at far left, was the son of prominent attorney Stillman Wightman and his wife, Clarissa Butler, a descendant of original settler David Sage. (Courtesy of the Cromwell Historical Society.)

IMAGES
of America

CROMWELL

Barbara Grotheer for
the Cromwell Historical Society
Foreword by Richard Franklin Donohue

ARCADIA
PUBLISHING

ISBN 978-1-4671-0270-4

Published by Arcadia Publishing
Charleston, South Carolina

Printed in the United States of America

Library of Congress Control Number: 2018953901

For all general information, please contact Arcadia Publishing:
Telephone 843-853-2070
Fax 843-853-0044
E-mail sales@arcadiapublishing.com
For customer service and orders:
Toll-Free 1-888-313-2665

Visit us on the Internet at www.arcadiapublishing.com

To the citizens of Cromwell, past, present, and future; to those who have worked to preserve town history; and to my family.

Contents

Foreword

One warm autumn afternoon, following a walking tour of Main Street with a group of basically interested high school students, one of them said the most remarkable thing to me: "[Historically,] Cromwell really has it all, doesn't it?" She was exactly right. Cromwell's economic and social history parallels that of the United States itself and could serve as a snapshot case study in any US history course. But that isn't ultimately what makes Cromwell and its history special.

What we have here is a place, a truly amazing place, that has lent itself to a myriad of incarnations: a bustling river port, a quiet farming village, a playful industrial hub, a healing city on the hill, a colossal rose garden, and yes, a perfect place to call home. And with prudence and respect for this place, our ancestors have ensured our love of and attachment to it by leaving it here for us. We can walk on the ancient brownstone walls along the Connecticut River; we can stand at the summit of Prospect Hill and see what John Adams described as the most beautiful land he had seen outside of Peacefield. We can still feel the pride and grandeur of an industrious community as we drive past the 19th-century Italianate homes on Main Street and gasp when we see the sun glistening off one of the country's largest ranges of greenhouses. It is all still here, and it is ours.

Over the past century, a few books have been published detailing life in Cromwell. The purpose of this one is to accomplish what I believe to be the most important task required of historians: to keep alive that which ought to be—and even wants to be—remembered. Not only do the images in this book represent the people and places of Cromwell, but through them, our Cromwellian ancestors speak to us and show us what they thought worthy of remembrance. May it strengthen or inspire your sense of being with this place called Cromwell.

—Richard Franklin Donohue,
Town Historian, Cromwell, Connecticut
President, Cromwell Historical Society

Acknowledgments

I would like to thank the Cromwell Historical Society for the opportunity to work on this volume. It has been a pleasure and a challenge. In particular, I am indebted to Richard F. Donohue, president of the society, for his breadth of knowledge and his unwavering support, patience, and assistance throughout the process. Maria Van Geystelen helped organize the final product. I am also appreciative of the efforts of past and present members of the historical society in collecting and preserving the many photographs and documents in their library.

I spent many days with the Elizabeth Maselli collection in the local history room of the Cromwell Belden Public Library, where the staff was unfailingly welcoming, enthusiastic, and helpful as I navigated the documents and the technology involved in researching this project.

Many generous people took time to contribute images and provide information. Unfortunately, I cannot mention them all. However, I would particularly like to thank George E. Landis for providing several new photographs and for his previous work with the historical society, Glen and Beth Johnson for spending several hours reviewing their collection of photographs and sharing memories, and Jean Dunning for guiding me through materials at the First Congregational Church.

I am deeply indebted to my friend and former colleague Cheryl Pease, who not only provided encouragement throughout but also read the material carefully and made valuable suggestions and corrections.

My thanks also go to Caitrin Cunningham, editor at Arcadia Publishing, for her guidance.

Colin, Nicole, Hannah, and Aaron have been a constant source of encouragement and joy. My enduring love and gratitude go to my thoughtful husband, Allan, who has been my sounding board, my first reader, and my very caring and patient supporter.

As a note of interest, the Mattabesset River has been referred to historically by several names, including "the Riverett," Little River, and Sebethe, along with various spellings of Mattabesset.

Unless otherwise noted, all images appear courtesy of the Cromwell Historical Society. Other contributors include the Cromwell Belden Public Library (CBPL), the First Congregational Church (FCC), and the Tournament Players Club (TPC).

INTRODUCTION

Nearly four centuries after its initial settlement, the town of Cromwell, Connecticut, has established enduring roots and made significant adaptations to meet the many challenges it has faced. The development of the town has been dictated by its location on the bank of the Connecticut River near the geographic center of the state. Bounded on the east by the river, on the south by the smaller Mattabesset River and extensive wetlands, and on the north and west by ridgelines, the community has always possessed restrictive physical borders.

Cromwell originated as a tiny religious and agricultural outpost of the larger colonial settlement of Middletown, which was granted extensive lands in 1651. As settlers began arriving in Middletown, some were given land "north of the 'Riverett,' " an area later referred to as Upper Houses or Upper Middletown. After some early transitions, about a dozen families remained to develop the land. These families built their homes on a small rise near the riverbank and began farming some of the outlying areas. By 1715, there were 50 households in the newly formed Northern Ecclesiastical Society of Middletown, or Upper Houses, a community that now boasted its own church and school. For over a century, the Congregational church and the town essentially shared a history.

As the village grew, numerous artisans began to contribute to the economy. Records show evidence of weavers, shoemakers, blacksmiths, coopers, tailors, tanners, potters, and carpenters. The riverfront became the center of economic life. Middletown itself gradually emerged as one of the busiest ports in New England. The Upper Houses community had its own bustling wharves and maritime industries. Ships' captains ventured forth to take part in the lucrative coastal and West Indies trade. The compact riverfront village expanded and became more prosperous with substantial homes and a growing merchant class. A few of the wealthier families owned slaves.

In the early 19th century, a trade embargo and the War of 1812 severely limited maritime trade, and the fortunes of Upper Houses declined. While some continued to pursue maritime activities and trade, the village generally reverted to its agricultural roots. However, by midcentury, the sleepy village was reinvigorated by the founding of several industries that were attracted by the accessibility of the river, and later, the railroad. The J. & E. Stevens Company became one of the largest manufacturers of hardware and iron toys in the country. Brownstone quarries were excavated by increasing numbers of Irish immigrants. In the early 1870s, Anders N. Pierson emigrated from Sweden and opened a greenhouse business. Within a few years, Pierson's greenhouses became the largest grower of roses in the country, leading to Cromwell's nickname of "Rosetown." His business encouraged the arrival of more Swedish immigrants. Italian immigrants settled in the larger city of Middletown, but many also moved to the community north of the Mattabesset River.

By the dawn of the 20th century, the citizenry had become more diverse. New religious denominations became part of the town's fabric. Business owners and executives built fine new homes along Main Street and contributed to the well-being of the town. Workers found housing on lower Main Street, in the Riverport area, or near the greenhouses. Many German immigrants established farms and businesses north of Evergreen Road. A few retail establishments supplied the basic needs of the growing number of residents. The Main Street business center, which began developing as the port declined, boasted a bank, drugstores, a small department store, several markets, and new gasoline and automobile repair shops, as well as the town government offices. Residents adapted to the sights and sounds of flourishing business and industry.

As new ethnic groups contributed to the cultural life of the community, political life also underwent a dramatic change. By 1850, Upper Houses had been struggling in its relationship with Middletown for 200 years. Geographic obstacles often made it impossible to maintain connections with the political and religious life of Middletown, so from its earliest days, the Upper Houses village was isolated and developed in its own fashion. Initially, having a separate church and schools was enough to accommodate the needs of residents, but by the mid-19th century, a stronger movement developed to become independent of Middletown. In 1851, the General Assembly of the State of Connecticut recognized Cromwell as a new town with a population of 1,259, according to census data. The origin of the town's name is murky, but it is generally conceded that it was named either for the 17th-century English leader Oliver Cromwell or for the privateer *Oliver Cromwell* that was built in the nearby town of Essex with crew members from Upper Houses. Numerous names were proposed, and Cromwell did not receive great support, but mysterious circumstances led to it being recognized by the state. With independence came new responsibilities and the need to organize a town government.

Despite the continuing presence of industry, Cromwell maintained its rural character well into the mid-20th century, with many active small farms. However, the post–World War II period brought more substantial changes to the town. As with other communities, a growing population became one of the first indicators of change. In addition, during the 1970s, Cromwell became the intersecting point for three major highways. Route 15 had been in existence for decades and passed just west of the town line. Two new highways, Interstate 91 and Route 9, sliced through substantial sections of the small town, isolating some areas and making others ripe for development.

The community struggled to respond to the accelerating changes brought about by development. Many new housing tracts rapidly ate up farmland. Some of the state's first condominiums dotted the hillsides. Retail centers went up near the highway ramps, threatening older, smaller, local businesses. Community planning became a necessity to contain chaotic development. New schools were built. A move from a single resident state trooper to a community police force was necessary to contend with increasing crime rates. The volunteer fire department required more people and equipment. Recreational facilities and social services strained to meet demand. By 1980, the population was 10,265, over three times the size just 40 years earlier, and the town was still growing. Newer residents were often commuters to Hartford, New Haven, and other cities; they needed town services, but initially, they seemed less invested in contributing to the town. For those citizens born prior to or shortly after World War II, the community where they had grown up was barely recognizable.

Despite all the difficulties, in time, Cromwell has adapted to its latest set of challenges, as it had previously. New businesses and new residents provide a larger tax base; long-range planning helps prioritize needs; expanded recreational, cultural, and social services improve the lives of many residents; a new format streamlines government. While older residents continue to provide historic continuity, more recent citizens have moved into leadership roles in political, educational, social, and civic organizations—and so, the cycle continues.

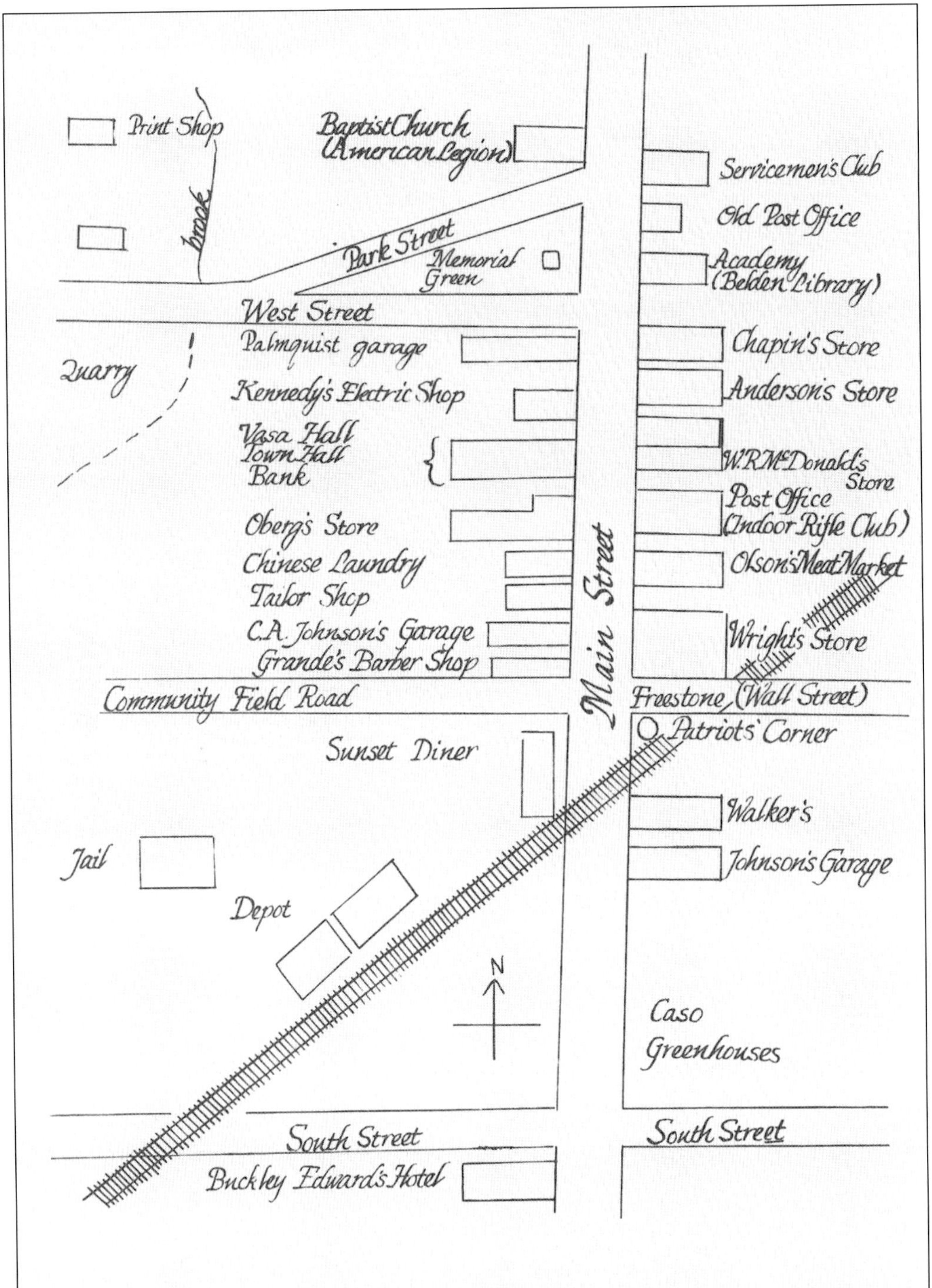

This map is a mid-20th-century attempt to illustrate the location of various enterprises in the Main Street business district, as they would have appeared in the early part of that century. Many of these businesses are pictured in the following chapters.

One

A Bustling Riverport

This tranquil view belies the major role that the Connecticut River has played in Cromwell's 370-year history. In the 1650s, the original settlers established their small village on its banks and depended on it for transportation and communication. Later, wharves and shipbuilding activity dominated the area. Still later, steamships and railroads loaded stone from local quarries. Frequently, floods disrupted lives, homes, and businesses. (Courtesy of George E. Landis, PPSA.)

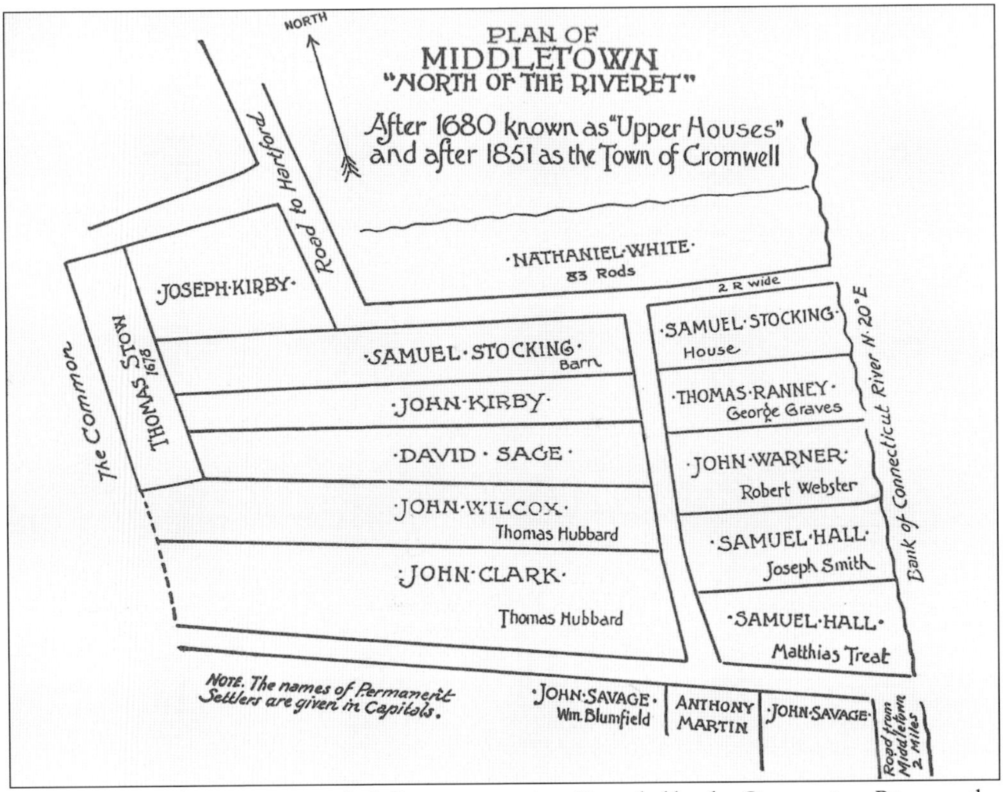

The original settlement was in today's Riverport section. Bounded by the Connecticut River on the east and the Mattabesset River to the south, the area included the present South Street, Pleasant Street, and Wall Street. Early properties ran directly to the river. The village, an extension of the larger Middletown community, became known as Middletown Upper Houses. Residents relied on subsistence farming for survival.

The "Little River," now the Mattabesset, and its marshland separated Upper Houses from Middletown. A ferry was established to bring residents to Middletown for worship and other gatherings. Frequently, spring floods made this crossing more difficult or impossible. This geographic separation made inevitable the increasing isolation of the Upper Houses settlement from Middletown proper.

Religion was the foundation of life in the early Puritan community, and the inability to easily access a house of worship was unacceptable. Beginning in 1690, residents of Upper Houses began to advocate for a separate parish. In 1703, the General Assembly allowed Upper Houses to form the Second Ecclesiastical Society of Middletown, also known as the North Society. By 1715, the initial Congregational meetinghouse was built, and a minister was selected.

In 1715, the Rev. Joseph Smith began serving as the first minister of the North Society in Upper Houses. In addition to a church, the new parish built the home shown here for Smith and his large family on Pleasant Street. Smith served until his death in 1736. Later residents included William Greaves and his wife, Celestia Hubbard, seen in this late-19th-century photograph.

Another early task of the new parish was to establish a cemetery. Previously, burials took place in Middletown. The new cemetery was created in the Timber Hill area in January 1713, with the earliest burial that of Martha Gipson, who died in February of that year. In the 1970s, Elizabeth Maselli made it her mission to preserve the graves and the records of burials at the Old Burying Ground. (Courtesy of George E. Landis, PPSA.)

Thomas Ranney, one of the first settlers of Upper Houses, became a substantial landowner and an influential member of the community. He died in 1713 at age 97 and was the only original settler buried in the Old Burying Ground. His 10 children continued his legacy. Beginning in the early 20th century, Ranney descendants and others associated with early settlers held reunions in town and contributed to its historical heritage. (Courtesy of George E. Landis, PPSA.)

Thomas Ranney's lands were divided among his many descendants. Eventually, his grandson Willett Ranney received 90 acres in the Timber Hill area, built this house around 1727, and farmed the land. Now on Bellaire Manor, the house is recognized as the oldest existing home in Cromwell. After his father's death, Willett Ranney Jr. occupied the house for a short time and then sold it to Solomon Sage, another prominent citizen, whose descendants lived there until 1882.

Built around 1745, Capt. John Stocking's house on Pleasant Street is one of Cromwell's earliest surviving homes and the oldest in the Riverport area. Captain Stocking, one of the first Upper Houses sea captains, was active in the coastal and West Indies trade. About 1744, he built two wharves and a warehouse at the foot of South Street, which marked the beginning of commercial development in the area. (CBPL.)

Wall Street resident Capt. Ralph Stocking was the last of the deep-sea sailing captains in Cromwell. Born in 1830, he was still engaged in coastal trade in 1884 with his schooner, which he docked at the end of Wall Street. He was also a coal merchant. He was a direct descendant of Samuel Stocking, an original settler in Upper Houses, and of George Stocking, a founder of Hartford.

Approximately 150 residents of Upper Houses served in the American Revolution, among them Jonathan Stow Jr., who served with Capt. Jared Shepherd's company. Jonathan and two of his brothers died in the war. They were direct descendants of Thomas Stow, another early settler.

Capt. John Pratt served in the American Revolution. In 1793, he purchased the Benjamin Butler homestead on Coles Road. Among other activities, he had a shop in the Riverport and served in the state legislature. When General Lafayette visited the area in 1824, Captain Pratt was his escort. This portrait of Pratt by artist Ralph Earl hung in the family home.

Capt. Nathan Sage commanded several ships during the Revolution and, as a privateer, seized many British vessels. He was honored on the floor of Congress for his contributions to the war effort. Captain Sage purchased the former Rev. Joseph Smith home in the Riverport, owned a shipyard nearby, and operated a tavern.

This portrait by artist Nathaniel Wales of Huldah Ranney Sage, wife of Capt. Nathan Sage, represents the many women of the town whose names and images were lost to history. These women remained in the village, taking care of children, homes, and businesses while their husbands ventured out on ships for war or trade. Captain Sage named a 279-ton ship the *Huldah* in honor of his wife.

Capt. James Riley lived on Prospect Hill and was active in the West Indies trade. In 1815, his brig *Commerce* hit a reef off the coast of Africa. He and his crew were captured by Arabs and spent several months as slaves in the desert until the US government paid a ransom for their release. *Sufferings in Africa*, Riley's book about his ordeal, sold one million copies.

William C. Redfield was a self-educated and intellectually curious resident who became a distinguished scientist. He opened a general store on Main Street and was one of the early members of the local debating society. In the 1820s, Redfield observed the behavior of hurricanes and published a paper on wind patterns of the storms. He published other papers on meteorological topics, many of which provided essential information to the US Weather Bureau.

In addition to his scientific work, William Redfield developed steamboats, ferries, and safety barges. One steamboat, the *Commerce*, seen in this drawing, was built in New York, launched in 1825, and initially operated on the Hudson River towing a safety barge for those passengers concerned about boiler explosions. Later, the boat traversed the Connecticut River. Redfield and his partners also had three freight barges built in the shipyards of Upper Houses.

Abijah Savage, a descendant of original settlers John and Elizabeth Savage, was a captain in the French and Indian Wars and in the American Revolution. He ran an important shipbuilding business on River Road, possibly assisted by some of his 14 children. An early advocate of community separation from Middletown, he served as a director of the school district and as a representative to the Connecticut General Assembly. His home on South Street was destroyed by fire in 1983.

Sea captain Absalom Savage is an example of the prosperity available from participation in the West Indies trade from the busy Riverport in the early 19th century. He married Sally Wilcox, built a fine residence in the newly fashionable Main Street neighborhood, and had four children. Captain Savage died while at sea in 1821, probably of yellow fever. His descendants live in the family homestead to this day.

Ralph Buckley Savage, the eldest son of Absalom Savage, is surrounded by most of his 12 children in this photograph taken outside the family home during an 1885 family reunion. Ralph Savage operated a general store south of the Academy building, later the Belden Library, on Main Street. He served as a selectman, town clerk, and town treasurer. He was also an active member of the Congregational church.

During the mid-1800s, the major economic activity of the village moved away from the river. Later in the century, the character of the Riverport changed. Steamboats and trains replaced the earlier wharves and shipbuilding. This 1890 image shows the railroad depot on the river at far left with a train near the station and the steamboat docking area on the river. (CBPL.)

This brownstone on the riverfront, pictured in 1971, marks the remains of the old boat dock where the Hartford boat picked up passengers and cargo in the late 19th century. At that time, the main cargo was brownstone from nearby quarries for export and coal for import. (CBPL.)

The Meriden & Cromwell Railroad built a large coal bin on the river in 1885 for its use. The capacity of the coal pocket was about 200 tons. However, when the river flooded, the coal bin did as well. Later, A.N. Pierson purchased this coal pocket. Another coal bin existed near the Valley Railroad station on Main Street; that coal was used in the boilers at A.N. Pierson Company.

The "spring freshet" has been a fact of life for residents of the Riverport since Colonial times. Occasionally, serious flooding occurs. This 1913 image shows floodwaters on the corner of South Street and River Road, an area right on the waterfront and more frequently affected by high water. In the background are sheds used in fishing for shad and alewives, and a small salt shed. (CBPL.)

During the historic flood of March 1936, the Connecticut River crested at a remarkable 30.25 feet in Cromwell. This photograph shows the view looking southeast from West Street. Visible on the left are Cromwell Tavern, Hitchcock's Drug Store on the corner of Wall Street, Patriots Corner, and the large building formerly housing the Warner Hammer Company. Boats were needed to traverse the Riverport area and lower Main Street.

This view looking northwest during the 1936 flood shows spectators gathered on Main Street at the corner of West Street observing the floodwaters. Oberg's store is at far left, followed by Vasa Hall, which housed the town offices, Cromwell Savings Bank, the town green, and the former Baptist church.

Approximately 141 houses were destroyed or severely damaged by the flood. Residents of the Riverport area had to evacuate, many assisted by volunteer firefighters and neighbors. One fourth of the town population of 2,800 was displaced. Emergency shelters were established at Nathaniel White School, town churches, and the Grange. The townspeople united to assist each other in this crisis.

Flooding not only disrupted road transportation to Middletown, but also rail transport. The railroad depot on Main Street is pictured here with the tracks completely covered by water. These photographs recall how the early settlers of Upper Houses must have struggled to travel to Middletown even during a normal spring freshet.

In 1955, Hurricanes Connie and Diane drenched Connecticut with nearly 30 inches of rain within a week. Significant water damage occurred in Cromwell, as in the Wall Street image shown here. One of the last serious floods occurred in 1984 when rowboats were needed to evacuate the Riverport area and lower Main Street. Willowbrook Plaza was affected, and Route 9 was closed between Cromwell and Middletown.

The Connecticut River shad, the state fish, has provided food and income for hundreds of years. Each spring, shad migrate up the Connecticut River to spawn. In Cromwell, people like the Schreier family fished for shad, expertly boned it, and sold it locally and for export. This 1944 image shows containers of shad packed in ice near a shad shack on the river ready to ship to New York City. (CBPL.)

After World War II, the Navy established a naval reserve training station on the riverfront near the former docks and train station. After the Navy abandoned the station, it became the home of Connecticut Hardware for several years. Today, only the foundation of this large building remains. (CBPL.)

Two

A Quiet Farming Village

The early settlers were subsistence farmers who gradually became more prosperous as they worked larger tracts of fertile land beyond the immediate Riverport area. After the heyday of maritime activity, the townspeople returned to their agricultural roots. They managed a comfortable living on small farms. Despite having some important industries, Cromwell could be characterized as a mainly rural community during the century between 1850 and 1950. (CBPL.)

In the 1700s, farmers moved north and west. Jared Shepherd, a veteran of both the French and Indian Wars and the Revolution, built the first home on the corner of Shunpike Road and West Street. Later, the Seth J. and Seth Paddock families lived in this house. In 1900, Walter Paddock demolished the family home and built a new stucco residence.

For over 150 years, the corner of West Street and Shunpike Road was known as Paddock's Corner. Five generations of the Paddock family farmed the large tract of land. In the late 1800s, Seth Paddock operated a cider mill on the corner. The barn and its iconic silos were emblematic of Cromwell for decades.

By the early 1700s, the fertile land in the Nooks area was being farmed. This Stocking farmhouse on Nooks Hill Road was built in the 1880s, possibly by Josiah Belden for his sister Susan Stocking. Local legend says the house may be haunted by the ghost of Susan's first husband, who was angry that she remarried after his death. (CBPL.)

Several Cromwell farmers grew tobacco as a profitable cash crop. Beginning in 1912, Raymond Goodrich purchased many acres in the open, flat Plains area of town for growing shade tobacco. The business was later sold to Consolidated Tobacco Corporation. One of their barns for curing tobacco is seen here. Many young Cromwell residents took summer jobs picking or sewing tobacco leaves.

Late-19th-century communities struggled with ways to help the poor. One method was to establish town farms where the poor could live, work, and be supported by the community. In Cromwell, the town purchased the Henry Shultz farm on the corner of Evergreen and Willowbrook Roads in 1894 to be used for this purpose. It lasted until 1904 when it was determined that more vagrants than community poor were using the facility. Later, this property became the Hofmann farm.

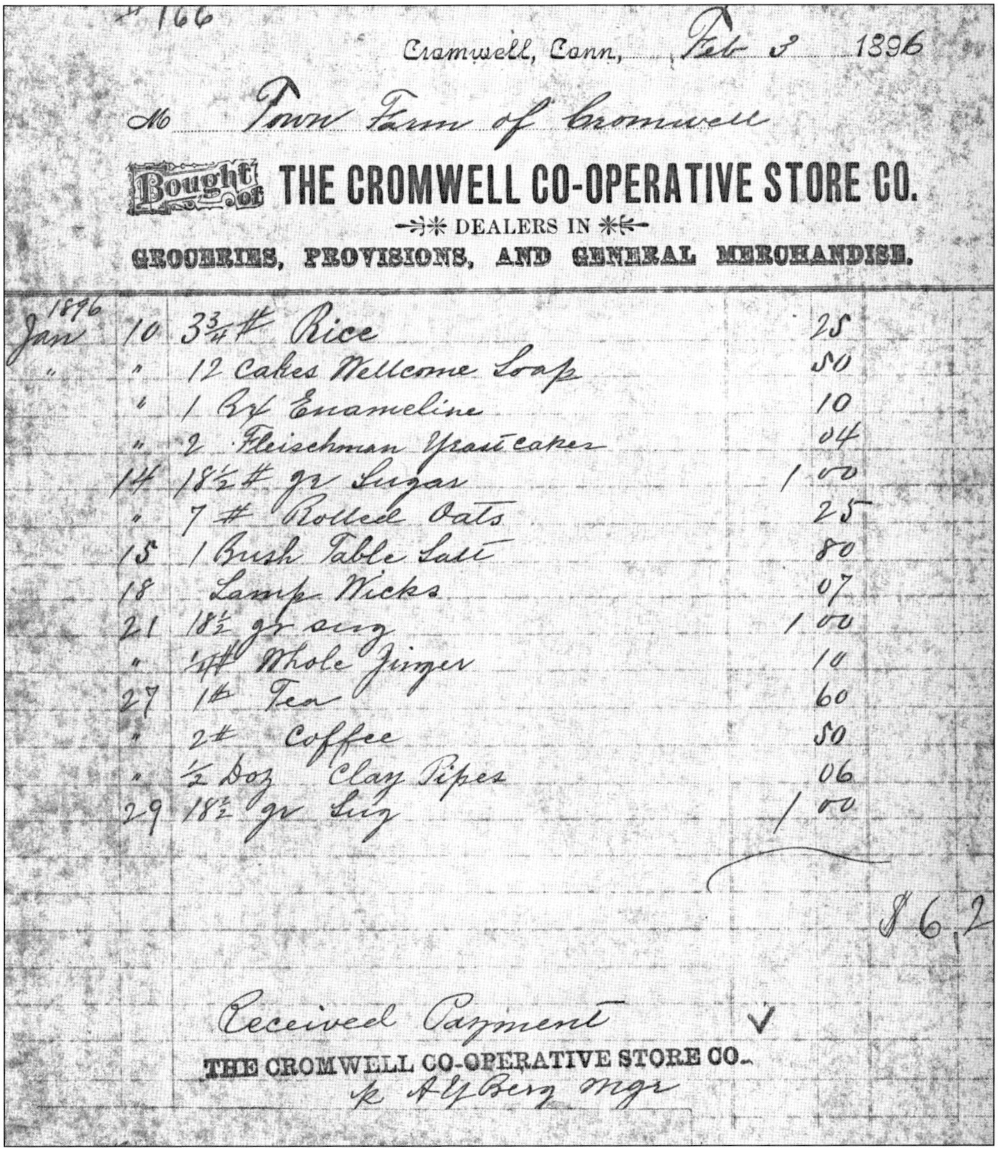

166

Cromwell, Conn., Feb 3 1896

M Town Farm of Cromwell

Bought of THE CROMWELL CO-OPERATIVE STORE CO.

DEALERS IN

GROCERIES, PROVISIONS, AND GENERAL MERCHANDISE.

1896 Jan	10	3¾# Rice	25
"	"	12 Cakes Wellcome Soap	50
"	"	1 Bx Enameline	10
"	"	2 Fleischman Yeast cakes	04
	14	18½# gr Sugar	1 00
	"	7 # Rolled Oats	25
	15	1 Bush Table Salt	80
	18	Lamp Wicks	07
	21	18½ gr sug	1 00
	"	¼# Whole Ginger	10
	27	1# Tea	60
	"	2# Coffee	50
	"	½ Doz Clay Pipes	06
	29	18½ gr Sug	1 00
			$6.2

Received Payment

THE CROMWELL CO-OPERATIVE STORE CO.

pr A G Berg Mgr

A receipt from the Cromwell Co-operative Store on Main Street dated 1896 indicates some of the provisions used by the town farm. Note the types and quantities of goods purchased, including such staples as coffee, tea, rice, oats, soap, and a large amount of sugar and salt. (Courtesy of Jane Morello.)

The Northwest Quarter of Cromwell was officially laid out in 1671, along with all the property near the Riverport, but the land here was rocky and less fertile. Because there was insufficient available land near the village center, some residents established small farms in this outlying district. Members of the William and Leona Sharp family are pictured at their farm on Coles Road around 1890. (CBPL.)

In 1925, John Monnes decided to switch to dairy farming after years of growing tobacco and potatoes on the 1869 family farm on Washington Street. The family cleared more land, purchased cows, and built new barns. One barn was built with lumber from the old quarry horse barns. The storage barn used lumber from the former Cromwell freight station. The Monnes dairy delivered milk daily to Cromwell residents until 1970.

In 1938, only two years after the destruction caused by the 1936 flood, Connecticut was hit by a major hurricane, for which the state was woefully unprepared. In Cromwell, more flooding occurred, and there was serious damage to buildings, trees, and crops. The roof of this octagonal barn, which was once in the rear of the Hubbard house on Main Street, was blown off and landed on another small building.

For most of the town's history, even those residents who had other sources of income often maintained a farm, but the economics of farming made this impossible by the late 20th century. In this 1971 photograph, Axel Anderson rides out on his tractor to feed his hens. The Anderson farm was on the corner of Hillside and Evergreen Roads. Today, this farmland is occupied by a residential housing development. (CBPL.)

Before the advent of town-wide sewer systems, rural communities and farms depended on privies. In the early 1970s, there were still many privies on properties throughout town, such as this one on Evergreen Road. However, by then, they were generally curiosities and historical artifacts, examples of a way of life fast disappearing. (CBPL.)

In the 1970s, there was still enough vacant land on Ranney Street to harvest a substantial truckload of hay. The Ranney Street and Timber Hill areas were home to some of the earliest farms in the village. Until the 1950s, much of the land in the neighborhood was used for potato farming, but post–World War II housing replaced much of that farmland. (CBPL.)

Three

Enterprise and Industry

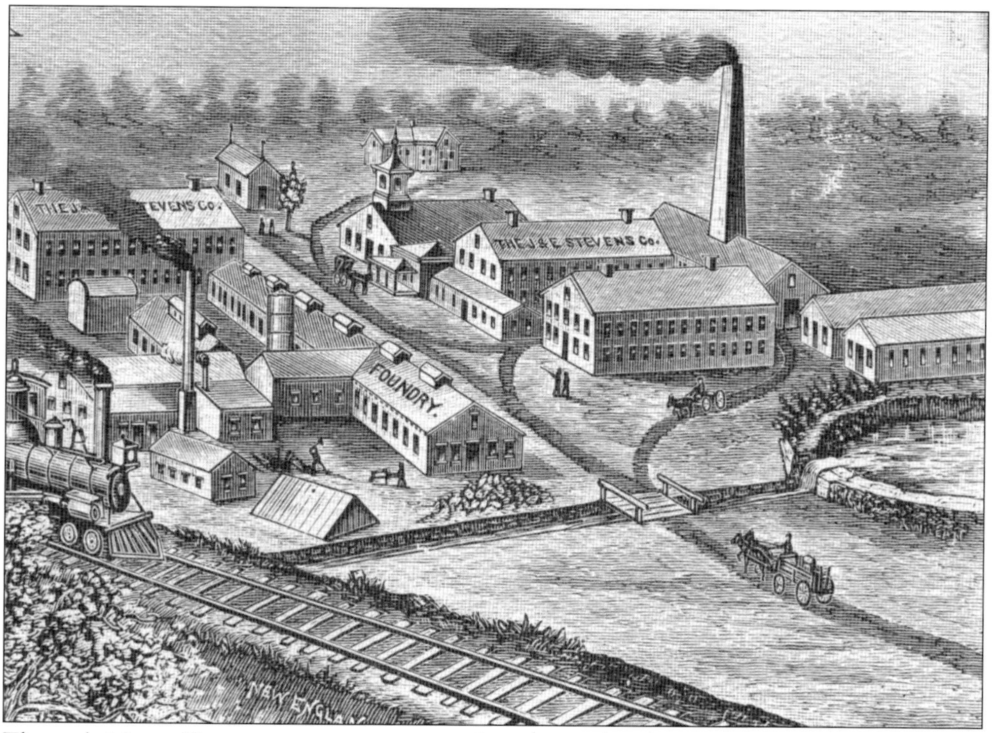

The early Upper Houses community attracted its share of tradesmen and artisans to serve the basic needs of the village. In the 19th century, several streams provided the water power needed for small factories to develop in Cromwell, as elsewhere. Arguably, the largest and most important of these was the J. & E. Stevens Company on Nooks Hill Road, seen in this drawing. Other significant enterprises developed throughout the town.

Israel Kelsey purchased land and a gristmill on Stony Brook in the Northwest Quarter in 1772 from Hugh White, who left town with other westward immigrants to settle in upstate New York. Kelsey's mill was profitable, enabling him to build a sawmill and a blacksmith shop on the property as well. His property became central to the development of this area of Cromwell.

Development in the Northwest Quarter led to the need for another cemetery. In 1802, Israel Kelsey donated land to the town for this use, reserving the right to pasture his livestock on the property. The first burial in this new cemetery was that of Aaron White, brother of Hugh and a veteran of the French and Indian Wars and the Revolution. (CBPL.)

William Allison moved to Upper Houses in 1845 and purchased a foundry in the Nooks near this pond, later known as Allison Pond. Various factory buildings are in the background. In 1846, Allison formed a partnership with the Warner brothers to manufacture hammers. The Warners left the partnership in 1849 to establish their own business, but Allison continued operating his factory successfully, producing excellent hammers marketed under several trade names.

John Dean Allison served as a lieutenant colonel in the Civil War and was wounded in the battle of Port Hudson. During the war, he carried a sword presented to him by the people of Cromwell. On his return, he ran the hammer business on Nooks Hill Road founded by his father. His sword and desk are now on exhibit at the Cromwell Historical Society.

Brothers Marvin and Isaac Warner purchased the Kelsey mill site on Stony Brook in the Northwest area. Their father did business in Middletown and is believed to be the first claw hammer manufacturer in the United States. The brothers went into partnership with William Noble in 1849. Their hammer manufacturing business became known nationally for the quality of the hammers they produced. All partners built large homes on Christian Hill Road near the business.

The original Warner Hammer plant was destroyed by fire in 1923. Under the leadership of Marvin's son, the factory moved to the center of town near Patriots Corner. At the new site, the company could use electricity instead of water power. Competition from less expensive machine-made hammers drove the company out of business at the beginning of the Great Depression. In 1970, Willis Warner displays his collection of Warner hammers. (CBPL.)

About 1843, brothers John and Elisha Stevens formed the J. & E. Stevens Company on Nooks Hill Road, shown in this early postcard view. By 1850, it was the largest industry in town. Although it began by manufacturing various hardware items, the company became highly successful and nationally known for its cast-iron toys and banks. The business expanded to encompass 11 buildings with about 120 employees.

His business success enabled John Stevens to invest substantially in the commercial section of Cromwell. He purchased the Savage Store on Main Street, erected another building adjacent to it in the early 1870s, and was part of the United Association group that built across the street. He was the first president of the Cromwell Savings Bank, town postmaster, and deacon of the Congregational church, as well as superintendent of the Sunday school. He died in 1892.

John Stevens erected this Italianate home at 395 Main Street about 1853. His wife, Cordelia, died in 1855, leaving him with four daughters. He remarried in 1856 and had five more children. In 1892, his widow sold the house to Russel Frisbie, a superintendent and designer at the Stevens Company. The home remained in the Frisbie family until 1969, when it was willed to the Cromwell Historical Society.

The success of the J. & E. Stevens Company made Elisha Stevens a wealthy man, and he was able to build a luxurious home on Main Street. He opened his own business, was a director of the Connecticut Valley Railroad, and served as Cromwell's postmaster from 1870 to 1876. Unfortunately, not everything went smoothly. Of his three wives, two died young. Bankruptcy in the 1870s created hard times for him. He died in 1889.

In 1868, Elisha Stevens left the family business to form the Stevens and Brown Company, manufacturers of tin and Britannia toys. The partners erected a three-story factory at the site of this waterhole behind the Academy building, visible in the rear. Initially, the business was highly successful. However, the Panic of 1873 led to bankruptcy. Stevens assumed the $100,000 debt and was eventually forced to sell his home and business. (CBPL.)

During his years of success, Elisha Stevens built this brownstone Italianate home at 385 Main Street at a cost of approximately $20,000. In 1905, the Women's Relief Corps purchased the building to house elderly war veterans. It remained in their hands until the 1950s, when it began its current role as a health-care facility.

Kate Ralph began working at the J. & E. Stevens Company during the Civil War when she was 16 years old. Each workday for 63 years, she walked a six-mile round trip to the plant and back from her family farm on Old West Street. This photograph, showing her painting one of the cap pistols that became a staple of the company business, represents the conscientious work of the many valuable employees of this legendary local firm.

Charles Frisbie joined the Stevens Company in 1877 and later succeeded his father, Russel, as superintendent. Charles purchased the company in 1912 and ran it until his own death in 1935. He was an active member of the Cromwell community, serving as director of the Cromwell Savings Bank, a state representative, and a state senator. He was also a prominent member of the Congregational church.

The Frisbie family had been associated with the Stevens Company in creative and management positions since 1866. The Frisbies maintained control of the company until 1940 when it was sold to a New York firm, which kept it operating until the 1950s. In 1948, a young woman poses in front of a still-active business. Today, Horton Brass, a maker of reproduction antique hardware, occupies part of the site.

In 1900, Edward Stevens Coe, an officer of the J. & E. Stevens Company, purchased this house on Main Street across from his uncle John Stevens. Coe's wife was the daughter of Ralph Savage. The home was one of many in the area owned by the prosperous businessmen of the time. Today, it has been remodeled and has a much different appearance than in the late 19th century.

Ruth Coe Pierson Dyer was a member of Cromwell's elite. The daughter of Edward Stevens Coe and Elizabeth Savage Coe, she married Frank Pierson, the son of Anders and Margaret Pierson. After Frank died at age 28, Ruth married Kirk Dyer. In this early-20th-century image, Ruth is shown near her home on Main Street with Valour Green behind her. (Courtesy of the Donohue family.)

Julia Waters Bryce, seen in this 1904 portrait, was the granddaughter of John Stevens. Her mother was Sarah Stevens, and her father was Joseph Waters, also an executive at the Stevens Company. The family lived in another new Italianate house on Main Street. Her father died tragically in 1868 after being thrown from his buggy on his way to work; her mother later married George Gillum.

This 1971 photograph of a signpost on Nooks Hill Road indicates directions to several businesses in the Nooks area. The sign has since been removed, and many of the businesses no longer exist, including the J. & E. Stevens Company. However, the sign is a reminder of the once economic importance of the area. (CBPL.)

The Connecticut Valley Railroad operated passenger and freight service from Hartford to Old Saybrook. On July 30, 1871, the first train stopped in Cromwell. The original station was behind the Academy but later moved to Main Street. By 1889, the Valley Railroad was a division of the New York, New Haven & Hartford Railroad. (CBPL.)

In addition to the railroad station near the town center, Cromwell also had a north station near the factories on Nooks Hill Road, such as the Stevens Company and Allison Hammer. This location was convenient for shipping and receiving of goods at these factories and contributed to the prosperity of the town.

The Meriden & Cromwell Railroad served Cromwell beginning in 1885. It brought manufactured goods from Meriden directly to the river in Cromwell where the freight was loaded on steamboats bound for New York. This image shows the station on River Road around 1886. While it began well, the railroad was not profitable, and the tracks were removed in 1904. (CBPL.)

The Meriden & Cromwell tracks ran along the Mattabesset River next to the present Route 372, behind today's Stop and Shop property, crossed Main Street south of South Street, and then turned left at the river to the station. There was a turntable on the corner of South Street and River Road on the property of the historic Joseph Frary house, pictured here After the tracks were removed, the turntable pit was not filled in until the 1960s. (CBPL.)

Quarrying was another important industry in Cromwell. The Connecticut Freestone Quarry on the corner of West Street and Timber Hill Road was the oldest of them, having opened in 1852. It had various owners, produced a high-quality brownstone, and provided jobs for many laborers. The quarry closed finally in 1906, about the time of this photograph, which shows One Allen Road on the hilltop.

The New England Brownstone Quarry was organized in 1886, taking over an earlier quarry operation on the site. It was located east of Main Street and north of Wall Street. Its property ran to the Connecticut River, seen in the background. It was the largest quarry in Cromwell.

The New England Brownstone Quarry, seen in this postcard view with a passenger train from the Valley Line passing by, had its own dock on the river north of the steamboat landing. There was a short railroad spur from the quarry to transport stone to the river. Thus, the old Riverport area was completely encompassed by railroad tracks and shipping activity.

Brownstone quarries ceased operation in Cromwell by World War I. The quarry holes became popular swimming areas for many years until they were contaminated by floodwaters in the 1930s. Later, they were perceived as a public nuisance. In 1970, Cromwell began the process of filling in the West Street quarry and gradually creating a public park with a playground and ball fields.

Joseph and Henry Petrofsky quarried traprock, a type of stone used in road building, on Berlin Road, now Route 372. The rock cliff is part of the site that Liberty Bank and CVS now occupy. The quarry, seen here after it closed, operated from 1925 to 1971. (Courtesy of George E. Landis, PPSA.)

Labor opportunities in the factories and quarries encouraged new workers to come to Cromwell. Irish immigrants were among the first to arrive. Later, Germans and Italians came as well. Most found housing near the river and on lower Main Street. Some homes housed several families and were in areas subject to flooding, as in this early-20th-century photograph of lower Main Street. The population of Cromwell increased and grew more diverse. (CBPL.)

The Clark brickyard began in 1897 in West Cromwell near the Sebethe Road area. Many Italian immigrants were employed on the site, which produced 45,000 bricks per day before mechanization. Homes for the workers were built near the business. The company donated bricks for the Northwest School and for the Masonic building on Main Street. The brickyard was profitable until the 1930s, when union difficulties caused it to declare bankruptcy.

Dr. Winthrop Hallock received his medical training at New York University and Long Island College Hospital with a specialty in treating nervous and mental diseases. After serving as a medical cadet during the Civil War, he became the assistant to the superintendent of the new Connecticut State Hospital in Middletown. However, he had a desire to operate his own facility.

In 1877, Dr. Winthrop Hallock opened a private sanatorium, known as Cromwell Hall, in this 1854 octagonal building with an octagonal barn and three acres of land on Prospect Hill. Patients were treated for a variety of emotional disorders. Mary Hallock, the doctor's wife, appears to have served as the matron of the institution and created a cheerful, optimistic atmosphere.

Dr. Frank Hallock, Winthrop's son, was born in 1861. After his father's death in 1898, he became the director of Cromwell Hall. He was also one of the founders of Middlesex Hospital, president and director of the Cromwell Savings Bank, president of the Belden Library Association, president of the Cromwell Cemetery Association, and a member of the school board. He died in 1937.

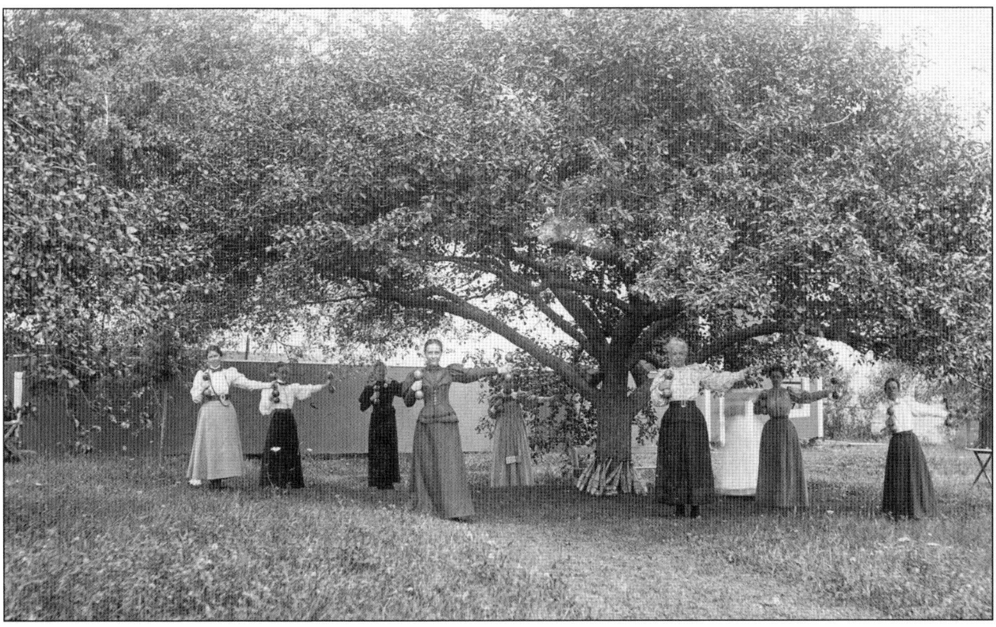

When Dr. Frank Hallock took over the medical care of patients at Cromwell Hall, he pioneered a more holistic course of treatment, including exercise, outdoor activity, massage, and diet, in addition to psychological therapy. The facility enjoyed great success; records indicate a movie star or two were among the patients. The extensive grounds were used for a variety of activities, such as this exercise group under the trees.

As Cromwell Hall became more successful, larger facilities were needed. This dormitory was built in 1909, but the building was destroyed by fire in 1957. Frank Hallock's nephew and his wife, Drs. Frank and Mildred Couch, operated Cromwell Hall from 1936 until it closed in 1956. In 1957, the property was sold to Holy Apostles Seminary. Today, it is Holy Apostles College, a Catholic liberal arts college and seminary.

Many of the members of the family associated with the operation of Cromwell Hall are seen in this undated photograph. From left to right are Dr. Frank Hallock; Susan Hallock Couch, supervisor of the nursing staff and kitchen; Dr. Mildred Couch; unidentified; Dr. Frank Couch; and William Couch, business manager and husband of Susan Hallock Couch. (Courtesy of the Donohue family.)

Four

A Proud Main Street

In 1802, a turnpike company received a charter to build a toll road from Hartford to Old Saybrook. The road ran through Cromwell, as shown by this Main Street milestone, and bypassed the Riverport district by straightening the main road from Wall Street directly south to the Little River. As maritime activity declined, new stores and homes appeared on Main Street to take advantage of the busy, improved roadway. (Courtesy of George E. Landis, PPSA.)

The small-town character of Main Street can be seen in a series of images. This c. 1900 photograph shows a vacant corner at Main and West Streets. A building known as the "Brown House," which was later moved to Wall Street, is at far left; the Baptist church is on the right. Behind the church is the Capt. Thomas Stow house, later demolished to build the Italian-American Club. (CBPL.)

In 1891, a group of prominent citizens erected a building on the west side of Main Street. Known initially as the United Association Building, it was located just north of Oberg's store. The first floor housed the Cromwell Savings Bank and town offices. The second floor was used for dances, meetings, and a poolroom.

John Palmquist's garage opened on the corner of Main and West Streets between 1900 and 1909, as automobiles became more popular. This photograph taken in 1914 shows the garage with the Brown House still at the left. The rooftop at far left is the United Association Building. By 1914, Palmquist had become partners with John Footit. The sign over the garage door reads, "Cromwell Garage." (CBPL.)

This 1905 postcard view shows the east side of Main Street. Chapin's Drug Store on the far left was Ralph Savage's store in the 1860s. John Stevens purchased the building in 1871 and built the larger attached building to its right, occupied in 1905 by Anderson's Grocery with Briggs' Hall on the second floor. Both buildings still stand. McDonald's store appears at center with the post office to its right. (Courtesy of Jane Morello.)

On January 31, 1909, the first trolley car arrived in Cromwell. A news article noted that about one thousand people lined Main Street to greet the trolley, which carried many state and local dignitaries. The Home Club gave a celebratory luncheon in the basement of the Congregational church. The trolley connected Cromwell to Hartford and Middletown until 1930, when it was replaced by buses. (Courtesy of Jane Morello.)

William McDonald arrived in Cromwell about 1873 and opened a general store on the east side of Main Street. His delivery wagon is pictured outside the store. McDonald was very active in community affairs. As a member of the state legislature, he promoted improved roads throughout Connecticut. (CBPL.)

During the winter of 1909–1910, a fire destroyed the McDonald store. The building had to be demolished, and this prominent location remained vacant for nearly 80 years. In the 1990s, a new building was erected that today houses a hair salon and an attorney's office.

This image of the Main Street business district, looking south from West Street, is from about 1910. The new trolley tracks are visible in the road at left. The former Stevens building is at far left, followed by the empty McDonald's store lot and other storefronts. On the right are the United Association Building and the new Palmquist Garage. (CBPL.)

This image from about 1910 shows the Main Street business district looking north. On the left is Oberg's Store, then the savings bank. The Baptist church is visible in the distance. On the far right is Wright's Drug Store. Wright's opened in the 1870s on the corner of Main and Wall Streets.

Millard Woodford Austin came to Cromwell in 1884 and purchased the meat business then run by Albert Briggs. He had a barn and smokehouse on the south side of Wall Street. Three delivery wagons supplied Cromwell, East Berlin, and Rocky Hill. (CBPL.)

In the 1920s, Grower's Store continued the long tradition of commercial establishments in this building, shown here in 1969. Among those owning or occupying the venerable site were Ralph Savage, John Stevens, Albert Briggs, and Charles Kirby. Today, an insurance company and a consignment shop do business there. (CBPL.)

This building served as the Cromwell Post Office between 1893 and 1926; information on the back of this postcard says that an indoor rifle range was upstairs. Before it was the post office, the building housed Hammer's Feed and Grain store. When the Masonic building was completed, the post office relocated there until 1962, when it moved farther north on Main Street to its present location. (CBPL.)

The Cromwell Cash Market, seen in this c. 1914 image, was located on the east side of Main Street near Wright's Drug Store. This market supplied meat to the community. W.S. Bailey managed the store while John Olson and his son made deliveries.

In 1926, the corner of Main and Wall Streets received a major renovation with the construction of a large brick building for the Masonic-Eastern Star Temple, which occupied the second floor. Hitchcock's Pharmacy, a First National Store, and the post office were early tenants on the first floor. In this 1970s image, ABC Pizza House, Bargains Galore, and L&S Communications occupy the building. Today, ABC Pizza has expanded, and Tea Roses Tea Room is a destination for many Connecticut tea lovers.

On the far left of this 1980s image, the still-vacant lot that was once the site of McDonald's store appears. The building in the center housed a tavern and Ziggy's Barber Shop, which occupied the former location of the Cromwell Cash Market. On the far right is the brick Masonic building.

Charles K. Ranney began operating a grocery store at One Wall Street in the 1880s. He is seen standing at left in the image above with John Barbour on the right. Ranney lived above the store. A century later, the location was occupied by the Bramble Bush café, seen in the 1971 image at left. Today, there is a pub in this location.

In 1889, August Oberg, a Swedish immigrant, opened a shoe repair shop north of the Academy building. By 1891, he was so successful that he was able to move to a larger location on the first floor of the Central Hotel across the street. Gradually, the shoe business became a well-known department store, and the Obergs purchased the building in 1924.

This photograph shows the Oberg store around 1900. August Oberg stands near the center of the group. Ella Footit is at left, and Rev. Nils Nielsen of the Swedish Church is at far right. The Obergs enlarged their store to encompass the first floor of the building and changed the hotel rooms above to apartments.

Nellie Oberg stands at right in front of the renovated storefront in this image from around 1930. Illness forced her father to retire in 1921, and Nellie ran the store until 1964 when it closed. The store was a Cromwell institution for over seven decades and is fondly remembered today.

Bulkley Edwards served as one of the original town selectmen and served several terms as the first selectman. He was a member of the board of assessors, moderator of town meetings, and a member of the General Assembly. In addition, he was president of the Cromwell Savings Bank and a major contributor to the Baptist church. Edwards was also one of the prominent citizens who encouraged political separation of the town from Middletown.

Bulkley Edwards ran the Tavern House, also known as the Edwards Hotel, at the corner of South and Main Streets, from 1836 until his death in 1896. It was built on the site of an earlier hotel owned by Edwards's father. The building contained the hotel, a tavern, and a bowling alley. The site is pictured in 1942. (CBPL.)

In 1874, the town built a small, brick, two-cell lockup for housing minor lawbreakers and tramps. The foundation of local brownstone is prominently seen here. The building was on the west side of Main Street near the railroad depot. It was used as a jail until about 1937, when it was sold for private business use. It has since been demolished.

The Valley Railroad served the town until 1948. The station on Main Street was purchased by Frederick Nordgren, who moved it back from the tracks and operated a feed and grain store there until the mid-1970s. Cromwell Hardware ran a store there for a few years. This photograph was taken in 1968. (Courtesy of Beth Johnson.)

In the late 1970s, Glen Johnson purchased the old depot and began the process of carefully restoring it for use as his real estate office. He restored the outdoor privy and brought in a caboose. Beth Johnson operated a gift shop within the depot for many years. There was also an ice-cream shop in the caboose. (Courtesy of Glen Johnson.)

Charlie Johnson operated a garage on the east side of Main Street, seen above. Later, he moved across the street with the Cromwell Motor Company and the Red and White grocery store, seen below, as neighbors. The first meeting of the new fire department took place in Johnson's garage in 1927. The wall of Oberg's store is on the far right. The buildings were on the corner of Main Street and Community Field Road. In 1966, these businesses were destroyed by fire. Mitchell's Restaurant occupies the corner today.

In 1956, Rodney McNeil took over Hitchcock's Pharmacy after Roy Hitchcock's death. In the mid-1960s, the face of Main Street was substantially altered after Oberg's Department Store closed. McNeil and a partner purchased the Oberg building and Vasa Hall and demolished them. A new commercial building and a parking lot replaced them. McNeil moved his pharmacy to the new building.

In 1928, the hometown Cromwell Savings Bank began construction of a new brick building on the corner of West and Main Streets. Upon completion, the bank moved to this new building and sold its former home, once the United Association Building, to the Order of Vasa, a Swedish-American fraternal and cultural organization. The site of the Vasa building is now a parking lot.

In 1971, the Cromwell Savings Bank celebrated its 100th anniversary. One thousand people attended the open house. William Buggie, bank director, at left, and Arthur Webster, bank president, welcomed people to the event. Bank employees dressed in period costume, and a dance band played. The refreshment table below was managed by, from left to right, Pat Bedlack, ? Kurdzil, Phyllis Ecker, Rita Barrett, and Edith McKnight. In 1974, the bank opened a branch office in the new Cromwell Square mall. The following year, the bank merged with Farmers and Mechanics Bank of Middletown. That bank has since merged with Citizens Bank, and the Main Street office is closed. (CBPL.)

The Georgian-style Wells-Hubbard house was completed in 1808 for use as a tavern. Located on the corner of Main Street and Nooks Hill Road, it served as a stagecoach stop on the new Middlesex Turnpike, part of the connection from Boston to New York.

In the 1950s and 1960s, more businesses began to develop along North Main Street. A new post office building opened in 1962. Next to it, another new building housed Liberty Bank, Cromwell Cleaners, and Marsal Realty. Today, the bank is still there, but Mario's Pizza has replaced the realty company, and Cromwell Cleaners has moved to a former bank building on the south side of the post office.

Sav-Mor supermarket also opened in the mid-20th century on North Main Street. It took over a building previously occupied by a bowling alley. Sav-Mor soon became popular for grocery shopping, and its lunch counter also offered a place for a quick cup of coffee, soda, or sandwich. Competition from several supermarket chains forced the store to close.

This showcase home near the Rocky Hill town line belonged to the Libera family. Shown in 1939, the home utilized the family concrete business for much of its construction. Today, Cromwell Concrete Products is one of the oldest Cromwell businesses. It supplies homeowners, contractors, municipalities, and states with a variety of concrete block and precast concrete products and is still family-owned and operated.

Other businesses operated on West Street near the Main Street center. In the early 20th century this barn, now demolished, housed the print shop of Burton Butterworth. It was located near a brook behind the Butterworth residence on West Street. In the early 19th century, Cornwall Doud Jr. owned the property and built a distillery there with his partner, Eben Wilcox. (CBPL.)

David Pierson emigrated from Sweden in 1909 to join other Swedish immigrants in Cromwell, and found work in the thriving greenhouse business. By the 1930s, he was married, had a son, and owned a house. He started an auto-repair shop next to his home at the corner of West Street and New Lane, which he operated for at least 25 years. In 1957, the garage was converted to Johnson's Grocery Store.

Johnson's Grocery was a popular store on West Street. Founded by John Johnson, it operated at 88 West Street from 1923 until 1955. After Johnson's retirement, his son and son-in-law continued to run the business but moved it to 72 West Street, a larger location and site of the former D.L. Pierson garage. The Johnsons sold the store in 1979; today, both locations are convenience stores. (CBPL.)

Many small grocery stores were located throughout Cromwell. Robert Clarke is seen in this 1970 photograph near the barn behind the home at the corner of Elm Road and Timber Hill. He is holding the sign for Swanson's Groceries, which once operated at that location. An article in the *Middletown Press* announced that Walter Swanson's store was open for business on April 3, 1936. (CBPL.)

The Cromwell Fire Department was organized in 1927, with Charles Johnson as the first chief. In 1929, the West Street firehouse, seen in this early view, was dedicated in the town center. The department had 40 volunteer firefighters and a brand-new fire truck. Nellie and Carl Thorell lived in the second-floor apartment and served as dispatchers for nearly 50 years.

Since 1891, town business had been conducted in the United Association Building, later Vasa Hall. Part of the building was leased to the town for use by the town clerk, the selectmen, a court, and for small town meetings. By 1949, this space was no longer adequate, and a new Memorial Town Hall was erected and dedicated on West Street opposite the town green and next to the fire station.

Five

Rosetown

The A.N. Pierson Company specialized in growing hardy, award-winning roses. It became the premier supplier of roses in the country and the second largest in the world. As a result, Cromwell became known as "Rosetown." This showcase rose garden, designed in 1915 and adjacent to the family home and business, is believed to be modeled after the garden in Elizabeth Park in Hartford, Connecticut.

Anders N. Pierson emigrated from Sweden and settled in Cromwell about 1872. He married, raised a family, established a world-renowned greenhouse and florist business, and contributed generously to the community. The family, pictured here, included Pierson and his wife, Margaret, seated, with daughter Emily at right. Standing behind are sons Wallace, left, and Frank. An unidentified young woman sits in front.

Anders Pierson married Margaret Allison Budde, a widow and daughter of the hammer manufacturer William Allison. They lived in her family home on Main Street and struggled to develop their business for several years. After the greenhouses became prosperous, they moved this house to New Lane and built a new home of their own on the Main Street site in 1892. Margaret Pierson was well known in town for her generosity and her many civic activities.

This c. 1930 aerial view indicates the expanse of the Pierson greenhouse campus. In addition, other extensive nurseries and farmland can be seen. Main Street is visible as the tree-lined diagonal across lower right; New Lane crosses the southern boundary of the greenhouses. Bartolotta greenhouses are at lower left. Today, much of this landscape is occupied by numerous housing and commercial developments.

Pierson encouraged Swedish immigrants to come to Cromwell. He provided employment and often housing as well. Here, workers load plants and flowers on the train at the local station. Pierson plants were shipped to New York and from there across the country and to other parts of the world. In the early 20th century, Pierson developed a trucking fleet for transporting his fragile flowers.

Pierson liked to have control over as many aspects of the business as possible and to provide consistent employment for his workers. He had a coal pocket, an icehouse, a trucking fleet, housing for workers, and the carpentry shop shown in this undated photograph. From left to right are workers Charles Nyren, William Blomberg, two unidentified, and E. John Johnson.

After the death of A.N. Pierson in 1925, his son Wallace ran the business successfully until his own death in 1946. Over the years, the Pierson business acquired considerable property throughout the town. By the 1930s, additional greenhouses had been built on the east side of Prospect Hill, as seen here. These greenhouses were later demolished and plowed underground.

Dr. Emily Pierson graduated from Vassar College and earned a master's degree at Columbia University. She spent several years actively involved in the Connecticut effort to win the vote for women. After the 19th amendment was ratified, Pierson attended Yale Medical School, graduating in 1924 when she was in her mid-40s. She practiced medicine in Cromwell for the next 40 years, also serving as the town director of health and the school physician.

Bartolotta Florist established greenhouses in Cromwell in 1933. They sold their flowers from a storefront on Main Street in Middletown, but the lease expired in 1951, so the family moved the entire business to Cromwell. Main Street addresses have been renumbered since then, but "Sta. 5" (Station 5) on this sign refers to the trolley stop in front of the business. (Courtesy of Edward S. Bartolotta.)

In June 1947, Edward S. Bartolotta graduated from eighth grade at Nathaniel White School. He is shown at the time in front of one of the family greenhouses on Main Street with his proud parents, Mike S. and Josephine Bartolotta. The family business continues to flourish today. Another family member has established Cromwell Growers, another greenhouse business that occupies much of the old Pierson property. (Courtesy of Edward S. Bartolotta.)

Many other greenhouse establishments operated in town during the 20th century, including Caso's at the corner of Main and South Streets. Luigi Caso began by growing vegetables for truck farming but later expanded to flowers. His sons continued to run the business until 1977. The greenhouses were torn down in 1989. Other important nurseries included Millane's, Leghorn's, Gardiner's, Scheu's, Pagano's, Branciforte's, and Smigel's. Most of their land has been sold to developers.

Six

A Suburban Town

By the 1970s, major highway construction changed the character of Cromwell. Both Interstate 91 and Connecticut Route 9, seen here in 1972, cut through the western part of town, simultaneously separating one part of the community from the others and creating enormous opportunity for commercial development. Cromwell struggled for years to adapt to the commercial and population growth created by the proximity of highway ramps. (CBPL.)

In 1970, the abandoned farmhouse of poultry farmer Leslie Wilcox was demolished to make way for a condominium development. Wilcox, a former first selectman, had worked on this land for decades. In 1964, he sold to Cornelius Millane and Marshall Gardner. They sold to Harry Gampel in 1968. The properties were strategically located off an exit from the newly constructed Route 9. (CBPL.)

By 1970, Harry Gampel's development company was well underway in the construction of the Cromwell Hills condominiums, a complex that would eventually number 524 townhouse units and be one of the first such developments in the state. Several other condominium developments were built in the community, which contributed to a substantial increase in population and the need for additional public services. (CBPL.)

In addition to a condominium complex, Harry Gampel constructed a strip mall next to the Route 9 interchange. The first phase of construction included a Grand Union supermarket and a Kmart. The second phase included several small retail stores, a restaurant, and a Farmers and Mechanics Bank. The sign at left indicates that the original design was for an enclosed mall, but that did not materialize. (CBPL.)

Irving and Mabel Johnson lived in this house at 207 West Street. During the 1936 flood, Mattabesset River waters inundated the open landscape in this area. Today, the Stop and Shop gas station stands at the former home site. There is extensive commercial development throughout the area. (Courtesy of Glen Johnson.)

Riverdale Cleaners was one of the early businesses to open along the developing Berlin Road commercial corridor. Lucy Berger and her husband, Paul, founded the business in the 1960s. Lucy was active in local politics and was the first woman to serve on the Board of Selectmen, beginning in 1975. The business continues under different ownership in the same location today. (Courtesy of James Marchio.)

The new commuter residents with growing families demanded more town amenities. A parks and recreation department was established in 1972 to take responsibility for existing recreational areas and to plan new areas and activities. Don Swanson was the first recreational director. Here, the Watrous brothers unveil the plaque honoring their father at the dedication of Watrous Park in 1986. Douglas Partridge stands at right.

As Cromwell grew, the fire department expanded to adequately protect the town. In 1966, the Court Street fire station opened, seen here. A third station was built 20 years later on Coles Road. In 2007, the original West Street station was replaced by a larger, updated facility. In addition to the chief, Cromwell currently has seven full-time firefighters and about 70 volunteers.

In the 1950s, Cromwell built its own high school and in 1960 opened Edna Stevens School for elementary students. Middle school pupils continued to attend Nathaniel White, but poor conditions there led to a substantial school building project. The high school was renovated to become a middle school, a new high school was constructed, and Nathaniel White was abandoned as a school. In the 1980s, the renovated building became Cromwell's town hall.

As part of the extensive project to build and renovate the schools and town hall, a new library facility, at left, was created as an addition to the town hall. The library moved from the nearly 150-year-old Academy building and was able to expand its services to the community. Another part of the renovation project included a home for a senior center and other town departments within the White building.

Seven

Faith and Knowledge

The first 150 years of town history were closely associated with the First Congregational Church. By 1840, the church had outgrown two previous buildings, and this Greek revival structure was completed on Main Street. The church recently celebrated its 300th anniversary; its congregation remains an active part of the community. However, by the 19th century, other churches were established in town. Education was important to the Congregational church, so schools were established early. (FCC.)

Rev. Edward Eells was the second pastor of the Congregational church, serving from 1738 until his death in 1776. He was a chaplain during the French and Indian Wars and was present during the siege and capture of Quebec. He lived with his wife on 11 acres granted to him by the church near the intersection of Ranney and Timber Hill Roads. His gravesite is seen at left. (FCC.)

The third pastor of the Congregational church was the Rev. Gershom Bulkley, a Yale graduate. He served the congregation from 1780 to 1808. He is described as an able preacher and a gentleman, but a very proper, aristocratic, and domineering man. He lived in this house at One Allen Road opposite the Old Burying Ground from 1778 to 1802. Later, the house was occupied by Bulkley's successor, the Reverend Joshua Williams.

The Great Hurricane of 1938 did severe damage to the town and to the church. Note the uprooted trees and the missing lantern tower that stood atop the church. Most of the old leafy trees along Main Street were completely destroyed by this storm.

As part of the national bicentennial celebration in 1976, the Congregational church chose to replace the historic church lantern tower that had been blown away during the 1938 hurricane. A successful fundraising campaign allowed the church to build the lantern and bring a crane in to raise it to its proper place. (FCC.)

In 1803, the new Baptist church erected a building on West Green near what is now St. John's Catholic Church. Frederick Wightman became the first full-time minister. In 1853, the building seen here was completed and dedicated on the corner of Main and South Park Streets. This church was active in the community until the late 1920s but was disbanded around that time. The building was sold to the American Legion in 1936.

This c. 1891 image shows three generations of Rev. Frederick Wightman's descendants. In the first row are Frederick Hartley Wightman and his new wife, Cecilia; seated in the second row are his grandparents Stillman and Clarissa Butler Wightman; and in the third row are his parents, Abigail and Frederick Butler Wightman. Unfortunately, young Fred died unexpectedly in 1894.

A Methodist congregation began meeting in individual homes in the 1820s. After the Baptists moved to their new building, the Methodists began meeting in the old Baptist church. In 1859, the Methodists erected their own church on Main Street where the Congregational church parking lot is today. They continued to use this building until the early 1900s when the congregation appears to have disbanded, and Bethany Lutheran Church took over the use of the building.

Beginning in 1892, attempts were made to organize a Lutheran church for Scandinavian immigrants. The efforts were successful in 1908 when Bethany Lutheran Church began meeting in the former Methodist church on Main Street. In 1965, a new church, seen here, was completed on Court Street, and the old building was sold to the Congregational church, which demolished it and used the land for a much-needed parking lot.

The first Catholics arrived in town in the 1840s. By 1876, there were 350 Roman Catholic residents, most of whom were Irish or German immigrants working in the quarries and the factories. In 1883, St. John's Catholic Church was completed on West Street near the West Green. The Catholic population increased dramatically over the next 75 years.

In 1953, as renovation and expansion of the old building began, St. John's was destroyed by fire. Services were held at Nathaniel White School until a new building was completed in 1954.

In 1892, A.N. Pierson donated land near his greenhouses on the corner of Main Street and Nordland Avenue for a Swedish Congregational church to be used by his many Swedish immigrant workers. In 1959, the congregation began the process of building a new church on the corner of Hicksville Road and West Street. The old church building was destroyed by fire in 1964, but the new building was not completed until 1965.

Comfort Ranney, a Revolutionary War soldier and descendant of an original settler, erected the left section of this building shortly before 1800. The first organizational meeting of the Cromwell Baptist Church occurred in this home. The Sage family later owned the property. In 1895, A.N. Pierson purchased it and donated the house and land to the Swedish Congregational church for use as an orphanage. It was expanded several times to meet the demand.

In 1915, the Swedish church dedicated a new orphanage on 27 acres purchased from Arthur Boardman. Known as the Hilltop, this orphanage provided educational activities and agricultural pursuits for the young people in its care. In 1972, this building was demolished, clearing the way for the Children's Home of Cromwell, now Adelbrook.

The land around the orphanage became headquarters for a large development of the Eastern Conference of the Covenant Congregational Church. The conference center on the hilltop had a tabernacle and numerous other buildings, including the dormitory pictured here in 1948. Later, Pilgrim Manor, a health-care facility, and Covenant Village, a senior housing complex, were built.

Initially, students of Upper Houses attended classes in Middletown or in private homes during winter months when not needed on the farm. By 1711, the town had its own school on the green, further contributing to the community's independence. By 1795, there were five school districts, including the Center School or Nooks School on Valour Green, pictured around 1895. In 1902, the building was moved to Nordland Avenue and became John Olson's meat market. (CBPL.)

Built around 1793, the small brick Plains School stood on Main Street. Although it was initially a one-room schoolhouse, a second room was added. By 1884, the school was very crowded with 103 students attending classes. When Nathaniel White School opened in 1902, most children moved there. The Plains School building was sold to the Knights of Columbus in 1938. After a fire destroyed the building, the Knights built new on the site.

One of the earliest town schools was on Coles Road in the Northwest District. In 1911, the older school, seen at left, was replaced by a new building sited on land donated by the Sharp family. The new school also functioned as a community center for the residents of West Cromwell. The building was used as a public school until 1959. Today, it has been renovated and is the Northwest Children's Center, a private daycare and preschool facility.

The Bell School was constructed in 1808 on School Street to meet the needs of the expanded Riverport area. The school had a cupola with a bell, thus its name. Josiah Belden was probably a student here. The building served as a school until 1902, when students attended the new Nathaniel White School. A few years later, the building was converted to a home.

By the beginning of the 20th century, the town's small elementary schools were overcrowded and in need of repair. In 1902, the Nathaniel White School was dedicated and named for one of the original settlers, who had left part of his estate to support public schools. Almost immediately, additional space was needed, so in 1905 the former West District School was moved and annexed to the rear of Nathaniel White, as seen here.

A seventh-grade classroom at Nathaniel White is seen in this photograph from 1925. To address continued overcrowding, the town erected a new building to the east of the original and similar to it in appearance in 1922. A corridor connected the two buildings. When students graduated from eighth grade, they were able to attend high school in Middletown if they wished.

In 1947, voters again approved an addition to Nathaniel White School. This time they added five classrooms, including a kindergarten, and a large all-purpose room, which was used as a cafeteria, gymnasium, and auditorium. In this photograph, students are eating lunch in 1950. Although the stage no longer exists, the room is still used as a town gymnasium and for other community activities. The kindergarten room is now called the Arch Room.

As part of its contribution to the town, the Congregational church built the Academy across from the church itself about 1834. The upper story of the building was for the exclusive use of the church, while the lower floor was used for literary purposes. It served as a higher-level school for the community, a venue for a debating society, and by the end of the century, as the local library.

Josiah Belden, born in Upper Houses in 1815, left town in 1831. He was a member of the first wagon train taking settlers to California in 1841. There, he became wealthy running a general store during the Gold Rush. He invested in San Francisco real estate. In 1888, Belden sent a substantial donation for the new public library in Cromwell. This painting is by local artist Elizabeth Savage Coe. (Courtesy of George E. Landis, PPSA.)

Daughter of Ralph Savage and descendant of Capt. Absalom Savage, Sarah Savage was a teacher of the eighth and ninth grades at the Academy. When the Belden Library was established at the Academy in 1888, she became the first librarian. Her original salary was 75¢ a week. She served until 1919.

The Belden Library Association managed the public library at the Academy building for nearly 100 years until the town took responsibility in 1985. A 1957 photograph of the library board of directors includes, from left to right, unidentified, Eleanor Coe, Dr. Frank Couch, Joseph Ruske, unidentified, and Lola Larson. Anna Strom, the librarian, is seated at the desk. The association continued to provide needed funding until 2011. (CBPL.)

Built between 1788 and 1816, this home on Prospect Hill is known historically as the Kirby-Wilcox house, named for two prominent 19th-century families. Between 1915 and 1957, the building was owned by Cromwell Hall. It has been in the Donohue family since 1957, when Cromwell Hall closed. It is currently the home of Donohue Music Studios and represents the numerous artistic and cultural opportunities in town. (Courtesy of the Donohue family.)

Eight

Community Life

By the late 19th century, the Connecticut River was no longer only a means of transportation and communication or a source of food. It became a recreational resource as well. A c. 1895 regatta is seen here, held on the river between Cromwell and Middletown. People also had the time for other leisure activities.

This area on the Connecticut River at the end of Nordland Avenue provided a sandy beach and a popular place for swimming. Nearby is the unique "blowhole," a geologic feature where one can hear the wind whistling eerily past the bluffs. Today, these bluffs are protected as part of River Highlands State Park.

In 1891, Carrie Savage married George Butler; both were descendants of early Upper Houses families. The bride appears in the center of this image surrounded by her attendants, from left to right, Julia Waters, Mary Waters, Susan Hallock, Carrie, Lucy Savage, Hattie Tucker, Bertha Smith, and Anna Coe (seated). In the 1930s, George and Carrie moved into the Savage family homestead on Main Street, and their descendants live in the house today.

When his sister Carrie married, George Savage gave her a horse as a wedding gift. George dismantled a buggy, put it back together inside the family home, and then brought the horse through the front door. Carrie found the horse and buggy inside when she returned to the house after the ceremony. George Savage is seen with his horse and sleigh in the rear of his family homestead around 1910.

Young members of the Wightman family and their Cromwell friends are shown picnicking in this 1890s photograph. The Wightman family lived in New York City, but they spent summers at their home on Main Street in Cromwell. They appear to have found many opportunities for amusement in the area.

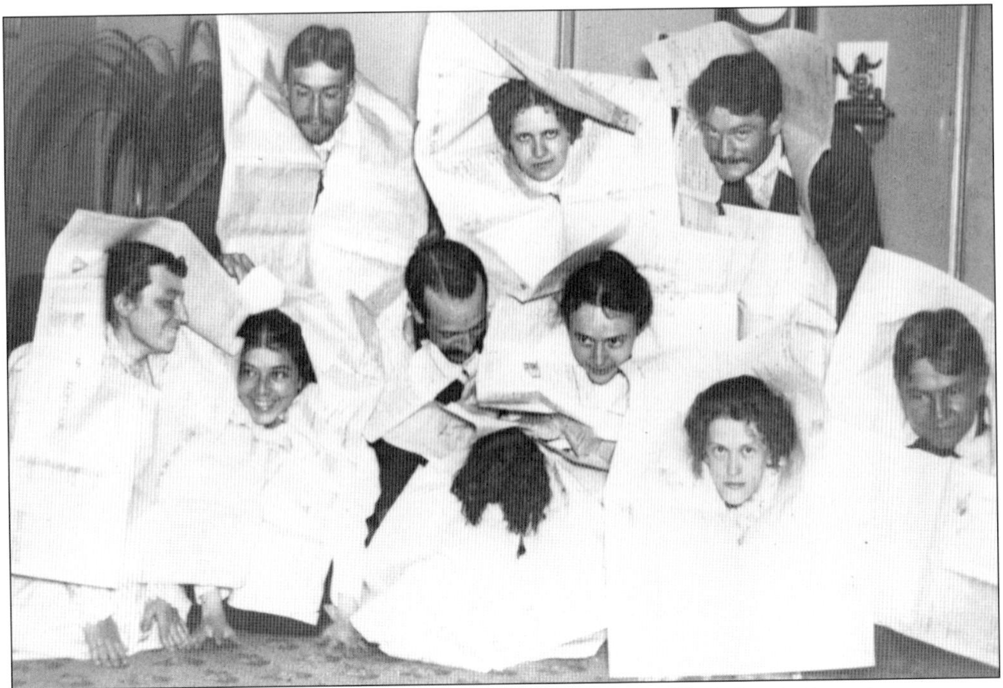

This amusing photograph, taken in the early 1890s, is labeled "flashlight heads through newspapers at Pryors." The young people are identified from left to right as (first row) Hattie Coe, Bess ?, Tom Barbour, Met Savage, Estelle ?, and Sam Marshall; (second row) Orrin Sage Wightman, Mary Botelle, and Russell Frisbie.

This photograph was probably taken on a Cromwell lane in the 1890s by Orrin Wightman. Bicycling had recently become a popular pastime. In the 1890s, bicycles had been newly designed to accommodate women. In addition, women also began wearing "bicycle bloomers." Young Met Savage displays both her bicycle, on left, and her bloomers in this image.

Briggs Hall was on the second floor of the Briggs Building, originally built by John Stevens and purchased by Albert Briggs in 1891. There was a stage used for various types of entertainments, such as seen in this undated photograph of a costumed cast posing on the stage. The sign posted on the right of the stage reads, "Spare the Rod, Spoil the Child."

During World War I, at least 114 Cromwell men served in the armed forces. The townspeople enthusiastically supported the war effort through fundraising and volunteer activities. On July 4, 1918, a one-mile-long parade was held in town to honor servicemen and to rally support for the war. It attracted nearly 5,000 observers. Floats were presented by many town organizations, such as this one from the Campfire Girls.

During World War II, Capt. Roy Hitchcock led the Home Guard in the Memorial Day parade in 1943. They are marching down West Street near Timber Hill Road. Hitchcock was the owner of a drugstore on the corner of Main and Wall Streets.

As part of the national air defense program during World War II, the Cromwell American Legion post established an aircraft warning observation tower at the top of Petrofsky's hill above West Street. Nearly 250 men, women, and children volunteered to man the site 24 hours a day. Young Lee Hitchcock is seen looking out the window of the tower in this image. A second site was near Timber Hill Road.

During the Cold War, the United States established several missile defense sites. This 1969 photograph shows the entrance to the Cromwell Nike missile site at the location of the previous World War II aircraft observation tower. The base was the radar and guidance unit for the actual missile launch site in Middletown. Today, the abandoned, overgrown property is behind the Country Squire condominiums. Various proposals for development of the area have been unsuccessful to date. (CBPL.)

After the quarry on West Street was filled in and became Pierson Park, a skating rink was popular there for several years, as seen in this image from the 1980s. An earlier skating area for townspeople was Moose's Pond on the corner of Court Street and Shunpike Road. However, a housing development was constructed on the former farm of the Moose brothers, and that pond is no longer accessible.

Cromwell residents have long been enthusiastic fans of and participants in many sports activities. When Cromwell built its own high school in the 1950s, the community showed strong support for the hometown teams. Here, coach Jake Salafia poses with his 1967 state champion basketball team, one of many championships that Coach Salafia and other Cromwell High teams have won in several sports. (Courtesy of Joseph Salafia.)

This Quonset hut from World War II was a fixture in the town center for over 50 years. It housed the local Boy Scout troop and was periodically upgraded. It was torn down in 1999 to provide space for the expansion of the police department. Scouting continues to be a popular activity for young people in the community. (Courtesy of Glen Johnson.)

Members of the Cromwell Grenadiers perform during a 1985 Memorial Day ceremony held on the Memorial Town Green. The Grenadiers, a junior fife and drum corps, were organized in 1972. They escorted the Cromwell Fire Department in many local parades and participated separately in fife and drum musters and competitions.

In 1928, Edgewood Golf Club opened near the river in Cromwell, seen here around 1930. Originally it was a private club, but by 1949, under the leadership of Andrew Pierson, it became semiprivate, opening to the public on a daily fee basis. Local residents took advantage of this opportunity.

In 1984, the Tournament Players Club purchased Edgewood and began a multimillion-dollar redesign and reconstruction of the course to a stadium design for accommodating major tournaments. Later, additional changes were made, such as the construction of the 12th green and fairway seen here. The location of the club provides spectacular river views. (TPC.)

Sammy Davis Jr. had a 15-year history of sponsoring a golf tournament with the Hartford Jaycees. In 1985, the Canon-Sammy Davis Jr. Greater Hartford Open was held at the upgraded Cromwell golf course for the second year. Davis is seen seated at right with tournament representatives. Today, a major televised PGA tournament occurs annually at the Tournament Players Club, attracting over 200,000 visitors to our small community. (TPC.)

Nine

A Sense of Place

In July 1905, the Society of Middletown Upper Houses dedicated a granite and bronze memorial to the "founders, fathers, and pastors" of Middletown Upper Houses, seen at left in this 1912 postcard view of Patriots Corner. The location, at the corner of Main and Wall Streets, is also called Stocking Triangle since it is on land once owned by Samuel Stocking, an original settler. In recent years, Cromwell residents have made efforts to recognize and preserve the community's heritage.

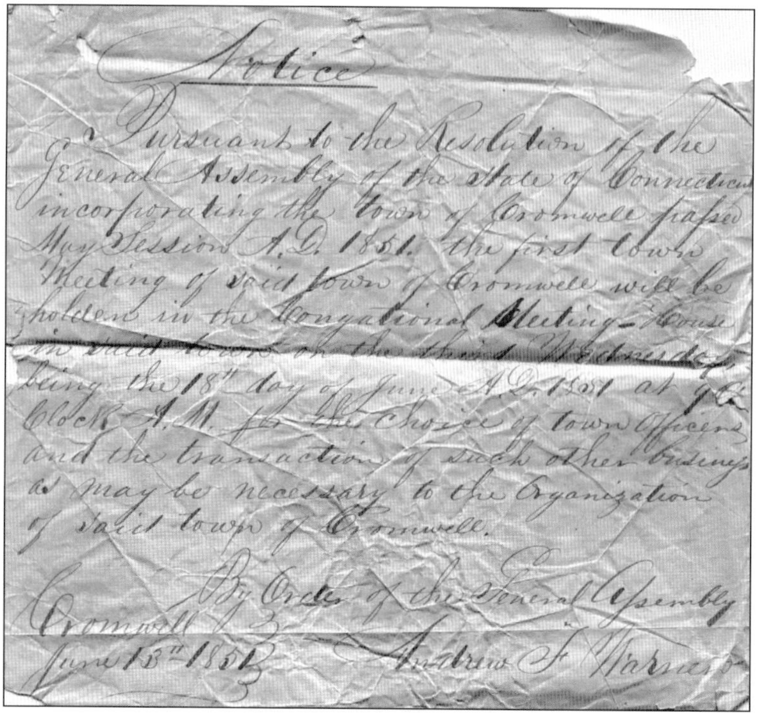

Notice

Pursuant to the Resolution of the General Assembly of the State of Connecticut incorporating the town of Cromwell passed May Session A.D. 1851. the first Town Meeting of said town of Cromwell will be holden in the Congregational Meeting-House in said town on the third Wednesday being the 18th day of June A.D. 1851 at 9 o'Clock A.M. for the choice of town Officers and the transaction of such other business as may be necessary to the Organization of said town of Cromwell.

By Order of the General Assembly

Cromwell
June 13th 1851

Andrew F. Warner

Cromwell became independent of Middletown by an act of the state legislature in 1851. This is the original notice of Cromwell's first town meeting to be held at the Congregational church on Wednesday, June 18, 1851, at 9:00 a.m., for the purpose of selecting town officers "and the transaction of such other business as may be necessary to the Organization of said town of Cromwell." (FCC.)

In 1908, Charles Collard Adams published a volume entitled *A History of Middletown Upper Houses*, containing both history and genealogy information about Cromwell. Here, he and his wife, Elizabeth Ranney Adams, are seated in the midst of family members gathered in 1910 to celebrate their 50th wedding anniversary.

At the instigation of local historian Charles Collard Adams, the Society of Middletown Upper Houses was created in 1903 for the descendants of the old families of Cromwell. Pictured are family reunion participants in 1905 posing at the gravesite of original settler Thomas Ranney. Charles Adams is the bewhiskered gentleman holding a hat standing at far right.

Members of the Carlson-Sjovall Post 105 of the American Legion place a wreath and gold star at the Cromwell World War I memorial on the town green during Memorial Day ceremonies in 1985. The memorial, designed by Boston sculptor Karl Skoog, was dedicated in 1925. Cromwell continues to hold its ceremonies on the traditional Memorial Day, May 30.

On July 3, 1974, townspeople gathered at Valour Green to open the bicentennial celebration by flying the bicentennial flag. In the photograph are, from left to right, Fred Frank (behind the flagpole); Dr. Simon Moore, chairman of the bicentennial commission (at the podium); Anna Doering, president of the historical society; Father Frank Liszewski, curate at St. John's Catholic Church; William Salwocki, first selectman; and Printice Toler, minister at the First Congregational Church.

Charles Frisbie, president of the J. & E. Stevens Company, stands on the grounds of his home around 1910. He inherited the house from his father and lived there with his wife, Emma, and their three children, Russell, Harry, and Mattie May. Tragically, both Harry and Mattie died of tuberculosis when they were each about 20 years old. At the time of the photograph, the home had undergone some renovation, including the addition of the veranda.

Russell A. Frisbie, son of Charles, was an inventor and designer who became president of the Stevens Company in 1935. His major contribution to the company was the design of a toy cap pistol, which became one of the most popular toys in the country. He is seen here in 1955 in the yard of his family home, which he willed to the Cromwell Historical Society.

Russell A. Frisbie was a talented inventor who particularly enjoyed working with motorcars. He built this car, seen outside the Frisbie home in 1906. Later, he founded a successful marine engine company in Middletown.

Harriet Coe Frisbie, wife of Russell Abner Frisbie, is shown in this undated photograph. She appears in a steam locomobile, which was purchased by her husband in New York City. It was the first automobile owned in Middlesex County. A.N. Pierson decorated the car for a parade in Middletown.

When the Cromwell Historical Society took ownership of the Stevens-Frisbie House in 1969, it began a program of cleaning, cataloging, and renovating. Grant money and donations helped fund the project. Much of the home interior is original, including the oak screens above the doorways. Today, the home provides exhibit and program space for the society.

Capt. Nathan Sage purchased the former Rev. Joseph Smith home on Pleasant Street and lived there for at least 10 years. This cupboard was in the dining room of the house. After the home burned in 1968, the cupboard was rescued and is now on exhibit in the Cromwell Historical Society.

A 1981 grant from the Connecticut Department of Economic Development and the Connecticut Committee for the Restoration of Historic Assets allowed the Cromwell Historical Society to carry out some restoration of the Frisbie barn and outbuildings on its property. Mildred Paddock donated some artifacts from the Paddock farm to place in the barn.

One of the major fundraisers for the historical society has been an annual barn sale. The first barn sale in 1970 offered some of the Frisbie possessions found in the house that the society did not need. That sale helped raise money for the restoration of the house. This view of an early 1980s sale shows the restored barn and many vendors and customers enjoying the day.

During the 1982 barn sale, a young entrepreneurial Richard F. Donohue raised money by shining shoes. Here, he is shown with longtime town clerk Bernie Neville on the grounds of the Frisbie house with Russell Frisbie's workshop in the background. (Courtesy of the Donohue family.)

Bake sales are dependable fundraisers for community organizations, and the historical society is no exception. The five women seen at this 1980s bake sale were particularly strong supporters of the society and its many events and programs. From left to right are Aline Babcock, Elizabeth Maselli, Ellen Groeper, Lois Donohue, and Marian Estra.

In the bicentennial year, the community honored town historian Elizabeth Maselli for her untiring efforts in preserving and protecting Cromwell's history. Her voluminous collections of photographs and documents are available at both the Cromwell Belden Public Library and the Cromwell Historical Society. In addition, she was responsible for restoring and protecting the historic Old Burying Ground. Douglas Partridge presented one of many awards for her service at ceremonies in 1976.

In the 1980s, the Main Street Historic District was listed in the National Register of Historic Places. A sign recognizing the area was donated by the Cromwell Junior Women's Club and posted on Main Street. From left to right on this occasion are Liz McInerney of the Cromwell Junior Women's Club; Lois Donohue, president of the Cromwell Historical Society; and Mary Amenta, first selectwoman.

In the 1980s, Cromwell began a nearly 30-year tradition of recognizing its past and conducting a town celebration. For years, the event was known as a Rose Festival or RoseFest. It featured several days of activities in the downtown center and Pierson Park, and attracted many participants. First Selectwoman Mary Amenta appears under the rose arch at an early festival. Elizabeth Maselli is left of the arch.

The Rose Festival evolved into the Riverport Festival with many activities centered on the waterfront in the new Cromwell Landing Park. Here, Civil War re-enactors, who held a weekend encampment at the park, enjoy some daytime refreshment at a booth on Wall Street outside Duffy's Tavern, site of the old Ranney store.

In 1935, Howard Hofmann began farming the land at the corner of Evergreen and Willowbrook Roads, site of the former town farm. He had cows, chickens, and horses. For years, Hofmann resisted those who wished to develop his attractive 78 acres. After his death in the late 1990s, the community organized to save this reminder of Cromwell's agricultural past. In 2001, the town purchased the land for passive recreation. Today, there are community gardens, a dog park, trails, and a spectacular view.

Today, Cromwell's River Road is bookended by two small parks. At the northern end of the road, the Rotary Club spearheaded a campaign during the 1990s to create the peaceful Cromwell Landing Park near the remains of the old boat docks and shipbuilding wharves. On the southern end, Frisbie Landing Park hosts concerts and a popular farmers market. Adjacent to Frisbie Landing, the Cromwell Outboard Association uses and maintains an attractive area. The historic waterfront continues to play a role in community life.

Bibliography

Adams, Charles Collard. *Middletown Upper Houses*. New York, NY: the Grafton Press, 1908.

Belletzkie, Robert J. "Cheshire Historical Society's Meriden, Waterbury, and Connecticut River Railroad, East, Ghost Tour from Cheshire to Cromwell." April 9, 2017.

cromwellbutlers.com.

Decker, Robert Owen and Margaret A. Harris. *Cromwell, Connecticut, 1650–1990: The History of a River Port Town*. West Kennebunk, ME: Phoenix Publishing, 1991.

Delany, Edmund. *Life in the Connecticut River Valley, 1800-1840: From the Recollections of John Howard Redfield*. Essex, CT: Connecticut River Museum, 1988.

Elizabeth Maselli Collection. Cromwell Belden Public Library, Cromwell, CT.

Johnson, Judith E. and William H. Tabor. *The History and Architecture of Cromwell*. Middletown, CT: The Greater Middletown Preservation Trust, 1980.

Perkins, Julia, Bernadette S. Prue, and Claudette Kosinski, eds. *Long Ago, Not Far Away: An Illustrated History of Six Middlesex County Towns*. Virginia Beach, VA: The Donning Company, 1996.

About the Organization

The Cromwell Historical Society was founded in 1964 by a group of individuals interested in the history of Cromwell, Connecticut, and the surrounding area. The membership is open to anyone interested in the history of Cromwell. Specifically, the society serves to collect, research, interpret, preserve, and disseminate information related to the history of Cromwell. The society maintains the Stevens-Frisbie House and three outbuildings located at 395 Main Street in Cromwell. The house serves as a museum of town history and a memorial to the Frisbie family. The buildings house a substantial collection of historical materials and artifacts that are preserved, maintained, and displayed by the society. The public is welcome to visit the house during museum hours each weekend between Memorial Day and Labor Day and on first Sundays throughout the year. In the spirit of disseminating history, the society presents an annual program series and special events throughout the year.

Cromwell Historical Society
Post Office Box 146
Cromwell, Connecticut 06416

Stevens-Frisbie House
395 Main Street
Cromwell, Connecticut 06416

www.cromwellhistory.org
www.facebook.com/cromwellhistory

Discover Thousands of Local History Books Featuring Millions of Vintage Images

Arcadia Publishing, the leading local history publisher in the United States, is committed to making history accessible and meaningful through publishing books that celebrate and preserve the heritage of America's people and places.

Find more books like this at
www.arcadiapublishing.com

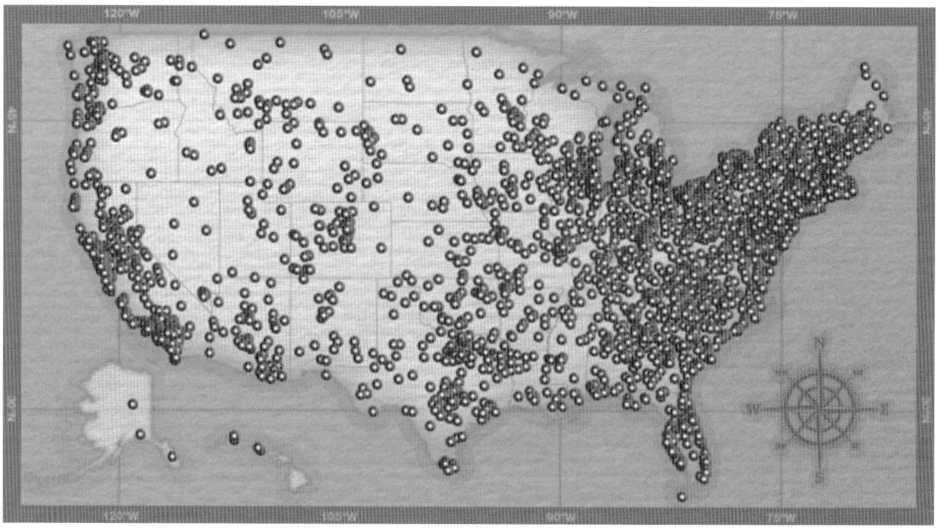

Search for your hometown history, your old stomping grounds, and even your favorite sports team.

Consistent with our mission to preserve history on a local level, this book was printed in South Carolina on American-made paper and manufactured entirely in the United States. Products carrying the accredited Forest Stewardship Council (FSC) label are printed on 100 percent FSC-certified paper.

MADE IN THE USA